QUIET MIND

QUIET MIND | A Beginner's Guide to Meditation

COMPILED AND EDITED
BY SUSAN PIVER

Shambhala

BOSTON & LONDON | 2008

Shambhala Publications, Inc.
Horticultural Hall
300 Massachusetts Avenue
Boston, Massachusetts 02115
www.shambhala.com

Revised and updated edition of the book *Joyful Mind: A Practical Guide to Buddhist Meditation* published by Rodale in 2002.

9 8 7 6

Printed in China
⊗ This edition is printed on acid-free paper that meets the American National Standards Institute z39.48 Standard.
♻ Shambhala Publications makes every effort to print on recycled paper. For more information please visit www.shambhala.com.
Distributed in the United States by Random House, Inc., and in Canada by Random House of Canada Ltd

Designed by Michael Russem, Kat Ran Press

Page 119 constitutes a continuation of the copyright page.

CONTENTS

THANK YOU

Josh Baran, Emily Bower, Duncan Browne III, Duncan Browne IV, Mark Butler, Michael Carroll, Adam Lobel, Melvin McLeod, Berkeley McKeever, William McKeever, Rick Rowe, Geoff Thurber, Emily Sell, Tami Simon, Eden Steinberg, Stephanie Tade, Andrew Weil, and all the remarkable teachers who shared their joyful minds.

EDITOR'S INTRODUCTION

We shall not cease from exploration
And the end of all our exploration
Will be to arrive where we started
And know the place for the first time.

T. S. ELIOT,
from "Little Gidding"

The practice of meditation is over 2,500 years old, and countless individuals have attested to its power to cultivate compassion and wisdom. Most recently, a growing body of scientific and medical research has shown that meditation can reduce stress, improve health, enhance performance, and measurably make us happier. Whether inspired by anecdotal or scientific evidence, more and more people are turning to meditation as a way of improving the quality of their lives. While some are looking for concrete health benefits, others feel drawn to meditation simply because they long for stillness and joy amid the pressures and challenges of daily living. This book-and-CD set is designed for anyone who wants to give meditation practice a try but doesn't quite know where to begin. This is the place!

WHAT IS MEDITATION?

As interest in meditation increases, so do misunderstandings. It would be really easy to get the idea that meditation involves having no thoughts and feeling blissed-out while sitting in a very uncomfortable position. Not so. All meditation involves is substituting for your thoughts another object of attention. Whether it is your breath, an image, or a sound, when the mind becomes absorbed in something other than thought, it relaxes. From this relaxation come many wonderful things, which you will discover for yourself if you make the practice a part of your life. So don't worry about clearing the mind of thought (which is impossible anyway), aspiring to any particular emotional state (meditation teaches you how to be comfortable with all emotions, even uncomfortable ones), or developing the ability to sit twisted up like a pretzel (sitting in a chair is fine, if you prefer). Meditation is the noble act of making friends with yourself. Breath by breath, moment by moment, you begin to learn who you really are. At first, this prospect may seem interesting, shocking, appalling, mysterious, or boring. Eventually, though, as you practice meditation, your mental chatter starts to quiet, and you find natural attunement with yourself. You breathe in and out. You notice the play of light and dark. Sensations rise and fall in the body and in the mind. Slowly, thoughts begin to settle, and you find that you are actually living in a very open and spacious world.

Meditation is often associated with Buddhism, and the practices contained in *Quiet Mind* are from the Buddhist tradition. The Buddha was simply a person who discovered a fundamental truth about being alive: To find lasting happiness, there is no need to be anyone other than who you already are. In fact, the core teaching of the Buddha is the importance of discovering this true self. Through meditation practice, you befriend your fear, restlessness, desire, shame, and dullness—those things that keep you from waking up to your natural state, which is already fully joyful, awake, and courageous.

The Buddha didn't invent meditation; it has been practiced in one form or another for many thousands of years—in fact meditation is understood to be our natural mind state to begin with. Therefore, it's not necessary to even think about becoming a Buddhist in order to practice meditation, just as it's not required to become a Christian to practice charity. These things are simply our birthright, the ground of being human.

A LITTLE HISTORY

Since the 1950s, the concept of meditation has become more and more familiar to Westerners. From Zen to Transcendental Meditation, from Tibetan to Korean to Burmese practices, various meditation traditions have made their way west and become familiar to us. We now see meditating monks in commercials for telephone service, and we find that a respected Buddhist teacher happens to be from Brooklyn or Melbourne.

Principles associated with meditation, such as mindfulness,

equanimity, and compassion, are being embraced by executives, filmmakers, and advertisers. Once viewed in the West primarily as a relaxation technique, we're now investigating the role of meditation in the treatment of depression and the repair of the immune system. But no matter how many marvelous applications it has regarding mental or physical health, meditation is primarily a spiritual path and was intended as such by the Buddha when he began teaching it.

If Buddhist meditation is new to you, it can be helpful to understand where it comes from. The starting point for all the practices in this book is the Buddha, who was born a prince in India in the fifth century B.C.E. His given name was Siddhartha Gautama, and he led a privileged and sheltered existence until, as a young man, he encountered the realities of sickness, old age, and death. These so shocked him that he renounced his wealth and position and committed himself to finding a way out of the suffering that all humans experience. He tried a lot of different methods, and after years of spiritual seeking, he finally decided to simply sit down under a tree in meditation until it all made sense, which it did one night, under a full moon in May, when he achieved enlightenment. The essence of his realization was this: Suffering is optional. He vowed to teach this truth to others.

It's interesting to note that as he was sitting in meditation under the tree, he wasn't *thinking* about the great questions of life, mulling over all sorts of explanations until he went, "Eureka, I've got it!" Instead of working harder and harder to understand, he relaxed more and more until the answer revealed itself. This is one way of thinking about meditation: that it is a profound relaxation of your conventional mind which then naturally calls forth the mind of wisdom. And since Siddhartha, a human and not a god, could do this, so can we.

The Buddha went on to teach about the path to enlightenment in India, but in the centuries that followed, Buddhism spread to Tibet, China, Southeast Asia, and Japan. Each time Buddhism arrived in a new country and culture, it changed somewhat, and certain teachings and practices were emphasized and others de-emphasized. As a result, today we have a variety of schools of Buddhism, including Tibetan Buddhism, Vipassana (also known as Insight Meditation, which comes from Southeast Asia), and Zen (which comes from China and Japan). These are the major Buddhist traditions practiced in the West today, and they are also the traditions studied and taught by the contributors to this book.

HOW TO USE THIS BOOK AND CD

Quiet Mind features six different sitting meditation practices presented by six renowned Buddhist teachers. Each teacher has written a chapter giving a brief overview of a particular practice. On the CD, they each offer guided meditation instructions so that you can try it out for yourself. Both the book and CD conclude by spotlighting yoga poses that support the body in sitting meditation. Also included are chapters on correct meditation posture, how to create a daily practice, and frequently asked questions, which anticipates the queries that come up at one time or another for most meditators, such as "How do I know if I'm doing it right?" and "What if my foot falls asleep?"

Please try these practices in any order that feels right to you. Here's a sampling of some of the ways you could use *Quiet Mind*:

• Select a meditation practice that interests you, read the essay on it in the book, and then listen to the corresponding audio track to try the practice. (A complete track list can be found at the end of the book.)

• Try a meditation practice from the audio program first; then read the chapter on it to enhance your understanding of it.

- Put the CD on and listen straight through to each meditation, noticing which practice or teacher you feel most drawn to.

- Sample each of the practices progressively, doing one practice daily for one week before moving on to the next.

If you find that one of the meditations or teachers interests you more than the others, there is a list of resources for further exploration at the end of the book.

If you want to practice meditation as a way of enhancing your mental and physical health, that's awesome. But if your aim is to know the true nature of reality, meditation can show you this, too—if you practice with discipline and commitment. So at some point, it's important to select one of the practices and commit to working with it for an extended period of time. This is the way the practice reveals its true essence and can genuinely transform your life. One warning: No matter how enthusiastic you are when you begin to practice, at some point *it will become boring.* This is actually thought of as a good sign. Though it sounds counterintuitive, when boredom rears its head, it's an indication that your conventional mind is running out of tricks. So hang in there! Interesting and beneficial things are just ahead. Please visit the aforementioned list of resources at the back of the book to locate a meditation teacher or center in your part of the world.

Each meditation in *Quiet Mind* is grounded in a lineage that is thousands of years old and the benefits have been touted by men and women, believers and agnostics, Westerners and Easterners. You can have confidence in them. That said, it makes no difference whatsoever to know how great these practices are unless your experience corroborates it. So be prudent. Check them out for yourself. The Tibetan meditation master Chögyam Trungpa Rinpoche taught that when we receive spiritual instruction, we shouldn't receive it uncritically. "Burn it, hammer it, beat it, until the bright, dignified color of gold appears," he said. He also wrote, "It is not enough to imitate your master or guru. . . . The teachings are an individual experience."

In that spirit, let your mind and heart wander through and resonate with these extraordinary teachings. Though they stem from different Buddhist traditions, each practice has exactly the same intention: to introduce you to your inherent wakefulness and joy. It is my sincere hope that these teachings will bring you happiness, freedom from suffering, true joy, and lasting equanimity.

MINDFULNESS OF BODY | How to Take a Good Posture

Although each of the practices included here offers a different way to meditate, there is one aspect they all have in common: taking a good posture. This doesn't mean sitting stiffly, as if someone just yelled, "Hey, you, sit up straight!" It means finding a way to sit that is both upright and relaxed.

The practice itself begins by sitting down. You can sit on the floor on a meditation cushion with your legs crossed, or you can sit on a chair or on the edge of a bed with both feet placed firmly on the ground. Though sitting on the floor on a meditation cushion may look more "authentic," sitting on a chair is just as good. The important thing is to take your seat with dignity and simplicity.

Next, make sure your back is straight but relaxed, like a tree. Trees move and sway in response to the wind, a flock of birds flying by, the sudden appearance of a rainstorm. Still, the tree points up with its branches and down with its roots. It is moving and not moving at the same time. Feel the crown of your head reaching up to the sky while your sitting bones reach down, to the center of the earth. This way, it's taught, you are joining heaven and earth simply by being a human being who is sitting down.

If you are sitting on a cushion, cross your legs loosely in front of you. If your knees don't touch the ground, you may want to

The posture of meditation, seated on a meditation cushion or on a chair.

support them with pillows. It is enormously helpful to have your hips higher than your knees. To do this, you might need to sit on more than one cushion, or on a cushion placed on the seat of a chair. Once your hips are higher, your knees and sitting bones can create a supportive triangle. If you're sitting on a chair, scoot forward a bit so that your feet are flat on the floor and your back isn't leaning on anything.

Your hands can rest comfortably at mid-thigh or just above the knees. It's also fine to rest one hand within the other at navel height, left within right, with the tips of the thumbs gently touching.

Unless instructed otherwise on the recording, keep your eyes open, gazing slightly downward to a spot on the floor that is four to six feet in front of you. Your gaze is soft, with the sense that vision is mixing with space rather than targeting anything specific.

Your jaw is relaxed, and your chin is basically parallel to the ground though slightly tucked to bring length to the back of the neck. Your mouth is closed with the lips very slightly parted. Shoulders and belly are relaxed.

Then, as you sit, begin to pay attention to your breath coming in and out through the nose. Your breath is always in the present moment; it can't be otherwise. So the simplest way to "be present" is to be with your breath. Sitting in this way is a basis for all the meditation practices that are to follow.

SHAMATHA | The Practice of Tranquility

SAKYONG MIPHAM

The untrained mind is like a wild horse. It runs away when we try to find it, shies when we try to approach it. If we find a way to ride it, it takes off with the bit in its teeth and finally throws us right into the mud. There is potential for communication and rapport between horse and rider, between mind and self, but the horse needs to be trained to be a willing participant in that relationship.

We train our mind with *shamatha* practice, the simplest form of sitting meditation. Shamatha is a Sanskrit word that means "peacefully abiding." Like all types of meditation, it rests upon two basic principles, known in Tibetan as *ngotro* and *gom*. Ngotro refers to "being introduced" to the object of meditation, while gom is "becoming familiar." In shamatha practice, we are introduced to and become familiar with the simple act of breathing. This is our object of concentration, the place we return to again and again when the mind has run off and we find ourselves clutching the horse's neck, hoping we won't end up too far from home.

WHY PRACTICE SHAMATHA?

Meditation is based on the premise that the natural state of the mind is calm and clear. It provides a way to train our mind to settle into this state. Our first reason for meditating might be that we want some freedom from our agitated mind. We want to discover the basic goodness of our natural mind.

To do this requires us first to slow down and experience our mind as it is. In the process, we get to know how our mind works. We see that wherever the mind is abiding—in anger, in desire, in jealousy, or in peace—that is where we also are abiding. We begin to see that we have a choice in the matter. We do not have to act on the whim of every thought. We can abide peacefully. Meditation is a way to slow down and see how our mind works.

The untrained mind is weak and inflexible. It lives in a zone of comfort. When the boundaries of that zone are challenged, it reacts by becoming more rigid. In contrast, the trained mind is strong, flexible, and workable. Because it can stretch beyond where it feels comfortable, it's responsive—not reactive—to challenges. Through shamatha, we can train our mind to be flexible and tuned in to what's happening now. We can apply this workable mind in all aspects of our lives including our livelihood, our relationships, and our spiritual path. So another reason to meditate is to develop a strong, supple mind that we can put to work.

It's easy to associate meditation with spirituality, because when we experience a moment of peacefully abiding, it seems so "far out."

Our mind is no longer drifting, thinking about a million things. The sun comes up or a beautiful breeze comes along, and all of a sudden we feel the breeze and we are completely in tune. We think, "That's a very spiritual experience! At least worth a poem or a letter home." Yet all that's happening is that for a moment we are in tune with our mind. Our mind is present and harmonious. Before, we were so busy and bewildered that we didn't even notice the breeze. Our mind couldn't even stay put long enough to watch the sun come up, which takes 2½ minutes. Now we can keep it in place long enough to acknowledge and appreciate our surroundings. Now we are really here. This has nothing to do with religion or a spiritual path. It has everything to do with simply being human.

PREPARING TO PRACTICE

The basic premise of shamatha meditation is "not too tight, not too loose." This holds true in every aspect of the practice—finding the right environment, preparing our body and mind to meditate, holding our posture, noticing thoughts and emotions, and bringing our mind back to the breath. The instructions are very clear, and we should follow them as precisely as possible. Some gentleness is also necessary, or else meditation becomes a way in which we're trying to measure up against a hopeless ideal. It's important not to expect perfection or get hooked on the finer points of the instruction. The practice takes consistent effort, and it can also be joyful.

One of the simple things that we can do is to create a good environment for practice—a place that is comfortable, quiet, and clean. A corner of your room that feels uplifted and spacious and private is a good enough place. It's unproductive to get caught up in chasing your idea of the perfect place to meditate. Some people from the city will go into the mountains to meditate in peace only to find that the crickets and the birds won't shut up!

Timing is also important. Decide on a regular time to practice each day, and try to stick with it. A ten-minute period in the morning is a good place to begin. The more consistent you can be in keeping to the routine, the better.

Planning is another element. It's better not to just sit down and hope for the best. If you plop down on your seat straight from the office or right after an argument, you may spend the whole session trying to slow down enough even to remember that you're meditating. If you're agitated, a slow walk might be in order. If you're drowsy, a cool shower before beginning the session might help. It can be inspiring to read a little about meditation first as a reminder of why you're practicing. Working with yourself in ways like this is intelligent and honest and can create the proper

Through shamatha, we can train our mind to be flexible and tuned in to what's happening now. We can apply this workable mind in all aspects of our lives including our livelihood, our relationships, and our spiritual path.

mind and body for good practice. But remember, preparation is not meditation; it is just preparation.

Half the challenge of meditation is simply getting to your seat. At the beginning of a session you may suddenly discover that you have more important things to do—housework to complete or phone calls to make or e-mails to write. One way to work with this kind of procrastination is to build a routine around preliminary stretching or walking before your session. This gives you a way to ease into it by softening your body and mind before you begin meditating. The more regularly you practice, the better you'll get at working with the strategies that the untrained mind cooks up to keep you from making it to your seat.

TAKING YOUR SEAT

You can use different postures for meditation, but under ordinary circumstances, sitting is best. Whether you're sitting in a chair or on a cushion, consider the meditation seat your throne—the center of your practice and your life.

When you sit down, take a balanced, grounded posture to allow the energy in the center of your body to move freely. If you're on a cushion, sit with your legs loosely crossed. If you're in a chair, keep your legs uncrossed and your feet flat on the floor. Imagine that a string attached to the top of your head is pulling you upright. Let your body settle around your erect spine. Place your hands on your thighs, in a place not so far forward that it begins to pull your shoulders down nor so far back that your shoulders contract and pinch the spine. The fingers are close and relaxed—not spread out in a grip as if you can't let yourself go. Tuck your chin in and relax your jaw. The tongue is also relaxed, resting against your upper teeth. Your mouth is ever so slightly open. Your gaze is downward, with the eyelids almost half shut. The eyes aren't looking; the eyes just see. It is the same with sound—we aren't listening, but we do hear. In other words, we're not focusing with our senses.

Slouching impairs your breathing, which directly affects the mind. If you slump, you'll be struggling with your body at the same time that you're trying to train your mind. What you want to be doing is the opposite: synchronizing your body and mind. When your focus is wavering, check your posture. Bring yourself back to the upright position. Imagine the string pulling your spine up straight, and relax your body around it.

WORKING WITH THE BREATH

Our minds usually jump wildly from thought to thought. We replay the past; we fantasize about the future. In meditation we place our mind on an object and keep it there. In shamatha meditation, the object is the simple act of breathing. The breath represents being alive in the immediacy of the moment.

Using the breathing as the object of meditation is especially good for calming a busy mind. The steady flow of the breath soothes the mind and allows for steadiness and relaxation. This is ordinary breathing; nothing is exaggerated. One simple technique is to count the in- and out-cycles of breathing from one to twenty-one. We breathe in, and then out—one. In and then out—two. Place your mind on the breathing, and count each cycle of breath. You can drop the counting when your mind is settled.

GATHERING THE MIND

As you focus on the breath, you'll notice that various thoughts and emotions arise. When this happens, acknowledge that you are thinking and return your focus to the breath. In focusing, you are bringing yourself back to attention. You are centering yourself in your mind and placing that mind on the breath. You are slowly settling. You're gradually slowing the mind. When you first begin to do this, the movement of thoughts may feel like a rushing waterfall. But as you continue to apply the technique of recognizing thoughts and returning your focus to the breath, the torrent slows

Having a mind that is at peace with itself,
a mind that is clear and joyous,
is the basis of happiness and compassion.

down to a river, then to a meandering stream, which eventually flows into a deep, calm ocean.

For the movement of the mind to slow down like this takes long, consistent practice. A good practice is one that we keep doing ten minutes a day, year after year. Through ups and through downs, slowly we become familiar with the natural stability, strength, and clarity of the mind. It becomes natural to return to that place. We let go of our conceptual ideas about it. We can relax there and enjoy it. We begin to let this natural state of basic goodness infuse our entire life.

Meditation practice predates Buddhism and all of the world religions. It has lasted through the centuries because it is direct, potent, and effective. If meditation becomes part of your life, please consider seeking further instruction from an experienced meditator. It might also be helpful to become part of a community of practitioners.

I have learned these instructions from my teachers and am glad to pass them on to you. May these instructions bring natural calm abiding into your life. Having a mind that is at peace with itself, a mind that is clear and joyous, is the basis of happiness and compassion.

DIANA CHURCH

SAKYONG MIPHAM is the leader of Shambhala, an international network of meditation centers founded by his father, the renowned Tibetan meditation master, Chögyam Trungpa. Recognized as the incarnation of the revered nineteenth-century Tibetan Buddhist teacher, Mipham Rinpoche, he is the author of *Turning the Mind into an Ally* and *Ruling Your World.* For more information, visit www.mipham.com.

VIPASSANA | The Practice of Clear Seeing

LARRY ROSENBERG

would like to share with you a two-part meditation. The first part is called *anapanasati*, which in the ancient Pali language of India means "breath awareness." It goes back about 2,600 years and was used by the Buddha to attain enlightenment. I learned it from Indian, Burmese, Thai, and Vietnamese teachers in Asia. The second part is called *vipassana* or "insight meditation." Anapanasati and vipassana have been practiced together for thousands of years; anapanasati naturally and easily gives rise to vipassana. The first practice calms the mind by focusing on breath. In the second practice, we release the focus on breath alone to focus on whatever arises.

The Buddha taught that there is so much unnecessary suffering in life because we don't understand ourselves very well. Would you like to get to know yourself? If so, sit down and take a look! Breath awareness is a way to do just this. Conscious breathing helps to calm and stabilize the mind so that it is fit to see into and understand itself.

To begin with, it's important to establish the body in a position or posture that's both comfortable and stable. Whether you're in a chair or on a bench kneeling or on a cushion sitting cross-legged, it is helpful for the body to be erect so that the head, neck, and spine are in a straight line, with the chin tilted down just ever so slightly. Good posture helps the body breathe properly and the mind stay alert.

Next, it's important to inhabit the body with awareness. Be sensitive to the fact that you're sitting. See if there is any obvious tension in the body. Common places where tensions accumulate for many of us would be the jaw, rather tight because we're determined. The shoulders may be hunched up, posed for action. Take just a few moments and move through the body with mindfulness, noticing any area that's contracted or tight, and, just for a moment or so, touch this area of the body with awareness. Probably it will relax a bit. It will soften.

You can keep the eyes closed with the lids fully shut or leave them half open without trying to see anything in particular. Put your hands on your knees or thighs, or clasp one hand inside the other.

Now you are ready to start observing the breath. It is helpful to take three or four deep breaths, a little bit deeper than your normal breathing. Then allow the breathing to assume its own rhythm. Let it flow naturally. You can rest your attention on the air coming in and out of the nostrils or on the rise and fall of the abdomen.

Insight meditation is the practice
of liberation: by making friends with
our old wounds, fears, anger, and loneliness,
we free ourselves.

Station your attention at either one, and watch each breath as it goes in and out.

Take it one breath at a time, giving full care and attention to each in-breath and each out-breath in turn, staying awake during the pause between breaths. Learn to allow the breathing to unfold naturally. If you find that you direct the breath—and most of us do at the beginning—simply observe this tendency to control. Such mindfulness will restore the natural flow of the breathing. This practice is not about attaining some special kind of breathing. It is not a yoga breathing exercise or breath therapy. It is an awareness practice, and what we are aware of is the sensation of breathing exactly as it is. You might find yourself straining or struggling. Notice that. When you do, the energy usually smoothes out.

As you practice, you'll find that from time to time you're not attentive to the breath at all. You have some other preoccupation about the past or the future. Perhaps you will get caught up in sounds or bodily sensations. As soon as you see that you are not in contact with the breath, very gently, very gracefully ease back to the in- and out-breaths once again. This coming back to the breath is without judgment, without blame, without finding fault. It's just coming back. It's important that you do this with gentleness because, as you begin to learn this method, you may have to do it a fair amount. If you practice, it gets easier. Attention to breathing will become continuous.

As the mind begins to calm down, it is fit to open up the second aspect of our practice, what is called vipassana or insight meditation. Insight meditation is a deep seeing into the nature of the whole mind-body process. It is a firsthand, direct way of coming to know ourselves as we truly are. In the Buddha's teaching, it is this clear seeing that liberates us from the suffering that we go through unnecessarily. In this next mode of practice, we retain focus on the breath as part of our method, but we loosen our grip a bit. Earlier, we were developing calm by attending to the breath exclusively; everything other than breath was considered a distraction. Now the breath sensations are not the sole object of focus. Now, we experience the breath as an anchor, helping us remain fully alert to our experience.

In vipassana, we learn to fully receive our experience—whatever it is—in an intimate and unbiased way. Just to sit, breathe, be ourselves, and see what is there. Nothing particular is supposed to happen. Whatever is happening is perfect. We learn to observe our experience without holding on to what we like or pushing away what we don't like. Thoughts, moods, emotions will come and go. The body will feel a certain way; these feelings will come and go as well. The same will be true of sounds and smells. What aspect of all this do you attend to? Let life tell you! Different elements of the process of mind and body will be distinctive, strong, vivid. They will naturally capture your attention. The challenge is to open to experience exactly as it is, with mindfulness. All the while, conscious breathing will accompany and support you like a good friend. In this second mode of practice, unlike in anapanasati, nothing is a distraction! Whatever we encounter is our life at that moment, and that is what we learn to be mindful of. Sensations will arise in the body. The practice is simply to bring awareness to those sensations. Can you become sensitive to bodily life without judging it? Not condemning what you don't like, not grasping onto what you do like. Sometimes the body will feel wonderful— meditative calm permeating the body with a wonderfully relaxed feeling. Can you let that happen without grasping it and trying to keep it forever? If you can't, you'll find that you suffer. See if that's true. Test it.

The same attitude applies to the mind. And when I say mind, I mean thoughts, images, and emotions—the different moods we go through, the likes and dislikes and fears and loves and loneliness that make up human existence. The mind grasps after things, holding them tightly or pushing them away aggressively. Sometimes the mind is confused, feels covered in darkness, is ambivalent and unresolved. At other times, it feels very fresh and clear. Can you let whatever is happening happen without preferring one state of mind over the other?

Insight meditation is the practice of liberation: By making friends with our old wounds, fears, anger, and loneliness, we free ourselves.

Just relax, breathe, and know what's there. Whatever is in you starts to present itself. This way of attending to your experience, watching its nature from moment to moment, from breath to breath, takes us to another dimension of consciousness, one which is spacious and silent. The silent mind is tremendously fulfilling. It is highly charged with life and touches the human heart deeply. You may find that you are wiser and kinder! Anyone who has tasted this emptiness no longer needs teachers or books to know its value.

Now it is important to learn how to work back and forth between these two modes of practice, calm and insight. As you're able to do so, sit and enjoy the show. Let it all happen, and stay awake in the midst of it. Be intimate with your experience. From time to time, as you find yourself caught up in thoughts, starting to analyze and psychologize, as the mind loses focus and gets lost in its own content, simply go back to the breath as an exclusive object of attention. Fine tune your attention with simple breath awareness, and either conclude the session that way or, if you feel your mind has calmed down, once again open the field to include whatever is there. It's sort of the right and left hands working together, helping to bring us to understanding and love.

Finally, a brief suggestion about a large subject: meditation in daily life. The Buddha's teachings are not limited to silent sitting meditation. We are encouraged to bring the mindfulness we develop while sitting to all of the activities that make up our lives. Bring undivided, full attention to every situation. If you are washing the dishes, wash the dishes. Notice if you get lost in thoughts about the past or future, thoughts that separate you from intimate contact with the activity of washing dishes. If you find yourself distracted, simply return to what you are actually doing. This suggestion applies to everything we encounter in our daily lives: eating, driving, working, waking up, and going to sleep. Nothing is left out. Start paying attention to how you actually live. Bringing alertness to daily life strengthens sitting meditation; sitting meditation enhances our sensitivity to daily life. Many of us have found this constant alternating between quiet contemplation and mindful action a beautiful way to live.

Larry Rosenberg practiced Zen in Korea and Japan before coming to Vipassana. He is the founder and a guiding teacher at the Cambridge Insight Meditation Center in Cambridge, Massachusetts, and a guiding teacher at the Insight Meditation Society in Barre, Massachusetts. He is the author of *Breath by Breath* and *Living in the Light of Death*. For more information, visit www.cimc.info.

ZAZEN | The Practice of Freedom

EDWARD ESPE BROWN

The meditation I offer is called *zazen* in Japanese. The instructions I'll present come from the Soto Zen lineage of Japan, which was established in the thirteenth century by the Zen master Eihei Dogen.

Zen practice is often associated with either koans or sitting meditation. In the Soto tradition, rather than using koans (such as, "What was your original face before your parents were born?"), we emphasize the posture and presence of zazen. In zazen, you sit down and spend time with yourself. You are not getting anything done or consuming anything. You are given a few basic pieces of advice, primarily about posture, and are encouraged to find out for yourself how to continue sitting. It's that simple—and that difficult.

The essentials are rather straightforward: Sit down and be quiet; find a way to sit up straight with fullness of spirit, and keep at it. Many things will happen. Let them. Zen suggests that the point is to experience your experience, rather than seeking to control it.

So whether it is on the floor using some cushions of your choosing, or in a chair, see if you can find some way to sit up straight without slumping, without leaning against anything. Study how to be balanced left to right and front to back. You are like a tree, growing to the heavens. See if you can find a balance between the effort needed to sit up straight and ease, the softness of mind and body associated with absorption.

We simply say, "Take your best posture." Because the body is a physical manifestation of consciousness, working on your posture is a direct, immediate way to work on your attitude, to work on your mind. You are allowing your body and mind to open, your vitality—chi and energy—to flow freely. You are unfolding. You are meeting life with the fullness of your presence. Rather than ducking or dodging, taking (unconsciously) the posture you (implicitly) believe is to your best advantage, you go ahead and embody the fullness of your body, of your being. You are liberated from your story. You are not so easily knocked over by life when you take this posture.

You will have many ideas about what meditation is supposed to be, and your experience in meditation will not match your ideas. You will believe that the important point is to get your experience to match your ideas of what your experience should be like. When you are unable to do this, you will say that meditation is difficult. You will be ready to give up. But when you can just sit, having the experience you are having, whatever it is, without comparing it to what it should be, you will have true ease. No longer busy

When you can just sit, having the experience you have, whatever it is, without comparing it to what it should be, you will have true ease.

chasing after some imagined perfection, you rest in the moment. You "own" your body and mind. In Zen this is called "No more worry about not being perfect." Welcome to being you.

Eventually, soon enough really, you will realize that what you are doing is maybe, possibly, probably not nearly as important as the way you do it, and you will start to consider whether there is some way to settle in, to settle down, to live the love you have in your heart and make it real in your life. Is there some way to be at home in this being I find myself being? To be at home in this body and this mind?

If you go to a Zen center, you may find that the forms of practice are presented quite strictly, but in the context of your own life, you can decide how strictly to do formal practice. You can also find many ways to simply stop in the midst of your life. For instance, I often do "coffee meditation" in the mornings, bringing a cup of coffee with me to my meditation cushion. While I sit quietly, from time to time I take a sip of coffee and thoroughly enjoy its robust fragrance and flavor. Similarly, you may find various places and times to sit quietly, gathering yourself together.

At the same time most people find that for meditation to have a significant impact on their lives, they need to make a commitment to a regular practice of sitting, whether it is at home, at a meditation center, or with a group of friends. You might find that sitting with others is inspiring and supportive.

You might be drawn to meditating first thing in the morning, or inspired to spend a few minutes sitting quietly before bed. Additionally there are dozens of resources that present instructions you might find useful (including those in this book and its companion CD). Go ahead. Try things out. See for yourself what fits with your life and engages your being. See for yourself what matters to you most deeply and if meditation of some sort helps you connect with that.

After twenty years of practice at the Zen Center of San Francisco where I became a disciple of Shunryu Suzuki Roshi—and more than fifteen years of practice since then—I have continued to find it useful to spend at least a few minutes sitting quietly each morning. Rather than worrying about how much you should practice or how perfectly you are practicing, it is more important to practice regularly. Do something you can commit to. Your life will change, because you have incorporated a life change.

Imagine: The bell rings to begin the period of meditation. You sit yourself down. You simply stop, sit down, and watch as you race across the internal landscape, driven to accomplish, driven to perform.

Keep watching. As you do, you allow yourself to breathe, to notice you are breathing, and, suddenly, you are at rest. You've come to rest and at the same time you are sitting with someone very busy figuring, analyzing, judging, aiming, progressing now forward, now back, and never arriving.

Finally it's okay to catch your breath.

KENT LACIN

EDWARD ESPE BROWN began cooking and practicing Zen in 1965 and was ordained as a priest by the renowned Japanese Zen master Shunryu Suzuki Roshi in 1971. He has been head resident teacher at each of the San Francisco Zen Centers—Tassajara, Green Gulch, and City Center—and has led meditation retreats and cooking classes throughout the world. He is the author of several cookbooks, including *The Tassajara Bread Book,* and is the editor of *Not Always So,* a collection of lectures by Suzuki Roshi. He is also the subject of the documentary, *How to Cook Your Life.* For more information, visit www.peacefulseasangha.com.

METTA | The Practice of Compassion

SHARON SALZBERG

All human beings are united by an urge for happiness. We want an experience that takes us beyond our small, separate sense of self; we want a feeling of being at home with ourselves and one another. At the root of even the most terrible addiction or violence lies this urge to be happy. It may be twisted or distorted by ignorance of where happiness is actually to be found—yet, that fundamental longing for genuine happiness is there.

The Pali word for lovingkindness is *metta*. The practice of metta helps us honor the urge toward happiness in both ourselves and others. We develop the ability to embrace all parts of ourselves: the difficult aspects as well as the noble. As we continue practicing from that base of inner generosity, metta gives us the ability to embrace all parts of the world.

Ultimately, metta overcomes the illusion of separateness. The unconditional experience of lovingkindness is a radical sense of non-separation. Thus, the nature of metta is to dissolve all the states associated with the fundamental error of separateness: fear, alienation, loneliness, despair, and feelings of fragmentation.

It's said that the Buddha first taught metta meditation as an antidote to fear. According to legend, he sent a group of monks off to meditate in a forest that was inhabited by tree spirits. The tree spirits resented the monks' presence, so they decided to scare them away. They transformed themselves into ghoulish visions, made terrible shrieking sounds, and created awful smells. The monks, appropriately terrified, fled the forest. "Please, Lord Buddha," they begged, "send us to meditate in some other forest."

The Buddha said, "I'm going to send you back to the very same forest—but this time, I'll give you the only protection you need." And so the Buddha gave the first-ever teaching of metta meditation. He encouraged the monks to recite the phrases that follow—but more importantly, to actually do the heartfelt practice of lovingkindness.

Like many such stories, this one has a happy ending. It's said that the monks returned to the forest and practiced metta. The tree spirits were so moved by the energy of lovingkindness the monks generated that they decided they quite liked them being there after all. They decided to serve and protect them.

Whether this parable is literally true or not, its inner meaning endures: A mind filled with fear can be penetrated by the quality of lovingkindness. Moreover, a mind filled with lovingkindness cannot be overcome by fear.

The beginning of metta practice is learning how to be your

May all beings be free from danger.

May all beings be happy.

May all beings be healthy.

May all beings live with ease.

own friend. As the Buddha said, "You can search the entire universe for someone more deserving of your love and affection than you are yourself, but that person is not to be found anywhere. You, yourself, more than anybody in the universe, deserve your own love and affection." Very few of us embrace ourselves in this way. Metta practice is the key to this treasure. Also, loving others without any love for ourselves tramples on healthy boundaries. So you begin by sending metta to yourself. The traditional practice uses a series of phrases, as follows:

> *May I be free from danger.*
> *May I be happy.*
> *May I be healthy.*
> *May I live with ease.*

If these phrases don't touch your heart, feel free to come up with your own. The important thing is not to recite the "correct" lines, but to use words that are meaningful to you.

From here, the practice proceeds in a very structured and specific way. After directing metta to yourself, you move on to someone you find inspiring or to whom you feel grateful. This person is called "the benefactor." Bring this person's presence into your mind, and direct the metta phrases to him or her:

May you be free from danger.
May you be happy.
May you be healthy.
May you live with ease.

Next, move on to a beloved friend, sending unconditional lovingkindness to that person in the same way:

May you be free from danger.
May you be happy.
May you be healthy.
May you live with ease.

The next person you go to traditionally is called "neutral." This is somebody you neither like nor dislike. If you have trouble coming up with a suitable neutral person, try thinking of a clerk you've seen at the supermarket or perhaps someone who walks his dog past your house. Again, use the same phrases you've used before, but this time directed to the neutral person:

May you be free from danger.
May you be happy.
May you be healthy.
May you live with ease.

Now you're ready to send lovingkindness to someone with whom you've had difficulty or conflict. To send lovingkindness to difficult or threatening people is not to forget about your own needs. It doesn't require denial of your own pain, anger, or fear. Nor does doing this practice mean you're excusing abuse or cruelty. Rather, you're engaging in the marvelous process of discovering and cultivating your inherent capacity for unconditional love. It doesn't have to do with being passive or complacent in terms of the other person; it has to do with your own spiritual expansion. Directing metta toward a difficult person leads to the discovery of your own capacity for lovingkindness that's born of freedom. And so you repeat:

May you be free from danger.
May you be happy.
May you be healthy.
May you live with ease.

In the final phase of the practice, we move on to offer metta to all beings everywhere, without distinction or exception:

May all beings be free from danger.
May all beings be happy.
May all beings be healthy.
May all beings live with ease.

In lovingkindness, our minds are open and expansive—spacious enough to contain all the pleasures and pains of a life fully lived.

In lovingkindness, our minds are open and expansive—spacious enough to contain all the pleasures and pains of a life fully lived. Pain, in this context, doesn't feel like a betrayal or an overwhelming force. It is part of the reality of human experience and an opportunity for us to practice maintaining our authentic presence. Every single one of us can cultivate lovingkindness and wisdom so that happiness becomes our powerful and natural expression of being.

SHARON SALZBERG has been practicing and studying in a variety of Buddhist traditions since 1970. She has trained with teachers from many countries, including India, Burma, Nepal, Bhutan, and Tibet. Since 1974, Sharon has been leading retreats worldwide. She teaches both intensive awareness practice and the profound cultivation of lovingkindness and compassion. She is cofounder and guiding teacher of the Insight Meditation Society in Barre, Massachusetts, as well as a cofounder of the Barre Center for Buddhist Studies. She is the author of several books including *Lovingkindness*, *Faith*, and *A Heart as Wide as the World*. For more information, visit www.dharma.org/ims.

TONGLEN | The Practice of Transformation

JUDITH LIEF

When the Buddha was a young child, he led a sheltered life, brought up in a wealthy family. His father was a regional king and, as such, officiated at ceremonies and state occasions. One of these annual celebrations was the planting festival, which took place when the farmers were about to sow the year's crops. It was a big event, and the local farmers and villagers would come from all around to celebrate.

At one of these planting ceremonies, when the Buddha was just a young boy, he was happily playing with his friends until he saw the plow go into the earth. As the plow cut through the soil and made a furrow, he became upset. The young Buddha was touched by how much life was disrupted and destroyed in the simple act of planting food. He saw the little bugs scurrying away from the plow and the worms cut in two. He saw lots of confused little grubs and other beings that were down below abruptly thrust to the surface and beings that used to be on the surface buried down below. As their world was flipped upside down, they seemed to be totally disoriented and unhappy. So many beings were suffering.

The Buddha was so struck by this experience that he left the festivities and sat by himself under a tree to think about what he had seen. It appeared to him that just to survive on the earth, we must inevitably cause other beings to suffer. No matter how kind we try to be, we cannot avoid it. Even the seemingly innocent act of growing food inevitably caused some beings to suffer and die.

That realization, which took place when the Buddha was just a boy, was like a seed that later ripened and inspired the Buddha to begin his personal search to understand the nature of suffering, why there is so much suffering in the world, and whether anything can be done about it. The awareness of suffering had touched his heart and awakened his kindness.

When we open ourselves to others, we are also opening ourselves to pain. As in this story of the Buddha, when we are aware of the suffering of other beings, as well as of our own suffering, kindness arises as a natural response. But we have a tendency to shield ourselves from pain and cover over that awareness. We reject those parts of our own experiences that are painful, and we also avoid facing the pain we see all around us. By distancing ourselves from pain, we distance ourselves from one another. We lose the ground of connection that makes kindness possible.

The only way to maintain that connection is to extend our awareness to include all of our experiences, not just the parts that we find comfortable. Meditation practice is a good way to begin because it is a process of becoming aware of whatever comes up in our minds, both good and bad, painful and pleasurable. We are learning to be open to who we are and whatever we are experiencing. So meditation practice is not just a mental exercise; it is a way of making friends with ourselves at a very basic level. Step by step we are learning more about ourselves and accepting and integrating those parts of ourselves we had rejected.

As we learn to accept ourselves, we are at the same time learning to accept other people. It may seem that there are always other people around and we have no choice but to accept them, unless we throw everyone out or become a hermit; but just putting up with people is not the same as accepting them. Acceptance is the tender and gentle process of opening our hearts to others, to ourselves, and to our common ground of suffering. Kindness begins at this immediate, personal level of experience.

By cultivating an attitude of acceptance and fundamental friendliness, we can lessen not only our own fear and tension, but also that of the people around us. We can actually shift the atmosphere in the direction of relaxation and kindness and in that way be a force for healing. To the extent that we are relaxed and open ourselves, the people around us begin to pick up on it.

It is like putting a drop of water on a blotter—one little drop just spreads and spreads.

We might prefer to ignore our tendencies to focus on our own concerns and foget about the concerns of others. However, if we want to cultivate kindness, we first need to understand our own selfishness. That is where we begin. We need to stop and take a good look at this fixation with ourselves.

Most of the time, we are so used to being selfish that we hardly notice it. Our self-interest is like a background noise we no longer hear. It is a constant buzzing that we cannot seem to shut off. As we go about our business, we are always asking, "What's in it for me? What's in it for me?" That undertone is there whether we are robbing banks or working in intensive care. Because of it, our actions always have a twist.

With children, selfishness is more on the surface. If you ask a child to cut two pieces of cake, one for her and one for her sister, it is likely that her piece will be a little bigger—or, if not bigger, it will have the icing flower on it. Clever mothers have one child cut the cake and the other choose which of the two pieces she wants. In that way you get surgically exact cake cutting.

By the time we are grown-ups, we have been told about sharing and we know better than to let our selfishness display itself so blatantly. This does not mean it is gone, however, only that we are more sneaky. We may just put one little extra particularly yummy-looking mushroom in our rice, or we might graduate to a more advanced form of selfishness and give away the best mushroom in order to bask in how virtuous we are.

Our fixation on ourselves may not be so crude; it could be as subtle as the unquestioned assumption that we are the center and all else is the fringe. Our approach is that although other people matter, we happen to matter a little bit more. If you look at a room full of people, chances are that each one has her little circle around her, of which she is the center and everyone else is the fringe. So everybody is looking out and checking back, looking out and checking back, each from her own little world. It is like a game I used to play with each of my daughters in which I would say, "I'm 'me' and you're 'you.'" Of course this game could go on and on forever because no one would budge from their position as the center of things.

The contemplative practice called *tonglen* in Tibetan, or "sending and taking" in English, works directly with the powerful tendency to focus on ourselves. The practice of tonglen exposes the depth of our self-absorption and begins to undermine it. It is a practice specifically designed to remove that obstacle and the many other obstacles that stand in the way of our natural impulse toward kindness.

Tonglen is sometimes described as a practice of "exchanging self and other." This is because the goal of tonglen is to flip that pattern of self-absorption around completely, to the point where instead of putting ourselves first, we put others first. Tonglen practice goes from the starting point of putting ourselves first, through the middle ground of viewing ourselves and others as equals, to the fruition of putting others before ourselves.

If our view is to focus on ourselves, then our actions will tend to feed that view by grabbing on to whatever builds us up and getting rid of whatever threatens us. Our habitual activity is to protect ourselves by constantly picking and choosing, accepting and rejecting—but in tonglen practice, once again, we reverse our usual approach. Instead of taking in what we desire and rejecting what we do not, we take in what we have rejected and send out what we desire—basically the opposite of "normal." Tonglen practice completely reverses our usual way of going about things.

Why in heaven would anyone want to do tonglen? For one thing, our usual way of going about things is not all that satisfying. In tonglen, as we become more aware of the extent of our self-absorption, we realize how limited a view that is. Also, self-absorbed as we may be, we cannot help but be affected by the degree of pain and suffering in the world and want to do something about it. All around us we see people suffering and, on top of that, creating more suffering for themselves daily. But so are we! In fact, we are they—that's the whole point. The confusion we see—that's *our* confusion. When we see all those people suffering—that's *our* suffering. We cannot separate ourselves from others; it is a totally interconnected web.

In tonglen practice we are cultivating the same tenderness of heart that started the Buddha himself on his journey to awakening. If we are losing heart, tonglen is a way of reconnecting with it. Tonglen has nothing to do with being a goody-goody or covering up our selfishness with a patina of phony niceness. The point is not to berate ourselves or force ourselves to be kinder. If we think we are not kind enough, it may not be that we are less kind than other people but that we are more honest. So tonglen begins with honesty and acceptance and goes on from there.

In the same way that it is possible to cultivate mindfulness and awareness through meditation practice, we can cultivate kindness through the practice of tonglen. Through tonglen practice we learn to work straightforwardly with the difficulties we encounter and to extend ourselves more wholeheartedly to others. Tonglen is training in how to take on suffering and give out love. It is a natural complement to mindfulness practice, a natural extension of the acceptance and self-knowledge that come as a result of sitting meditation.

Each time you practice tonglen, begin with a basic mindfulness practice, such as shamatha or vipassana as taught in earlier chapters. It is important to take some time to let your mind settle. Having done so, you can go on to the practice of tonglen itself, which has four steps.

The first step is very brief. You could think of it as clearing the decks. You simply allow a little pause, or gap, before you begin. Although this first step is very brief and simple, it is still important. It is like cracking the window to let in a little fresh air.

In the second step, you touch in with the world of feelings and emotions. Each time you breathe in, you breathe in heavy, dark, claustrophobic energy; and each time you breathe out, you breathe out light, refreshing, clear, cool energy. With each breath, the practice shifts direction, so there is an ongoing rhythm back and forth. You are taking the habit of grasping and rejecting, and you are reversing it.

In tonglen practice we are cultivating the same tenderness of heart that started the Buddha himself on his journey to awakening.

The third and fourth steps take that same approach and apply it to specific topics. Start as close to home as possible, with something that actually affects you personally. You should work with a topic that arouses real feelings, something that actually touches you or feels a little raw. It does not need to be anything monumental; it could be quite ordinary. For instance, maybe someone screamed at you when you were driving to work. You could breathe in the aggression they threw at you, and you could breathe out to that person a wish to free them from the pain of that anger. If you yourself have just come down with a sickness, you could breathe in that sickness and breathe out your feeling of health and well-being. The point is to start with something that has some reality or juice in your life.

Once you are under way, it is good to let the practice develop on its own and see where it takes you. In this case, no matter what comes up in your mind, you breathe in what you do not like and you breathe out what you do, or you breathe in what is not so good and breathe out being free of that. For instance, after you breathe in that driver's aggression and breathe out your soothing of that anger, what might come up next is your own anger at being so abused first thing in the morning when you had started out in a pretty good mood. You could breathe that anger in and breathe out the ability not to take such attacks so personally. In that way, your thoughts follow along naturally, revealing more and more subtle layers of grasping and rejecting.

In the fourth step, you expand the practice beyond your own immediate feelings and concerns of the moment. For instance, if you are worried about your friend, you expand that concern to include all the other people now and in the past who have had similar worries. You include everybody who has suffered the pain of seeing someone they are close to in danger or trouble. You breathe in all those worries and breathe out to all those countless beings your wish that they be freed from such pain.

Tonglen practice is a radical departure from our usual way of going about things. It may seem threatening and even crazy; but it strikes at a very core point: how we barricade ourselves from pain and lose our connection with one another. The irony is that the barricades we create do not help all that much; they just make things worse. We end up more fearful, less willing to extend ourselves, and stunted in our ability to express any true kindness. Tonglen pokes holes in the barricades we create.

Tonglen is always about connection: making a genuine connection with ourselves and others. It is a practice that draws us out beyond our own concerns to an appreciation that no matter what we happen to be going through, others too have gone through experiences just as intense. In tonglen we are continually expanding our perspective beyond our small, self-preoccupied world. The less we restrict our world, the more of it we can take in—and at the same time, we find that we also have much more to give.

JUDITH LIEF has been a Buddhist teacher for over twenty-five years. She was a close student of the Tibetan meditation master Chögyam Trungpa, who trained and empowered her as a teacher in the Buddhist and Shambhala traditions. Sakyong Mipham, his son and successor, recognized Judy as a senior teacher, or *acharya*. She has worked as executive editor at Vajradhatu Publications and dean of Naropa University, in Boulder, Colorado. The editor of several books by Chögyam Trungpa, she is the author of *Making Friends with Death: A Buddhist Guide to Encountering Mortality.* Judy divides her time between teaching, writing, and editing. For more information, visit www.judylief.com.

HEALING MEDITATION | The Practice of Peace and Joy

TULKU THONDUP

True healing or well-being is having peace and joy in our lives. The source of this healing is none other than our own mind. The mind is innately peaceful and joyful. Also, peace and joy are concepts created by the mind. So the most effective way to heal is to use the mind—both the right means and the source of meditation.

Although the mind is the source of healing, positive mental objects such as peaceful images have an important role, too. They enable us to tap into our mind's healing powers. For ordinary people like us—who function and sustain ourselves entirely on mental objects created by our habitual dualistic concepts, passions, sensations, and emotions—creating positive images is a powerful inspiration that inevitably leads to true healing.

When we see a mental object, our mind grasps at it as a real, truly existing entity. Once it grasps at an object, the mind starts a process of discrimination, classifying the object as mine or yours, as good or bad, as an object it likes or doesn't like, of wanting or not wanting, craving or hating. Such emotions bring feelings of sadness or excitement, pain or pleasure. The more intense our feelings and emotions, the tighter our mental grip of grasping. We lose our own birthright, the peaceful center within us, and become slaves of our mental objects, dependent on external circumstances.

Through meditation, we can realize the awareness of the peaceful and joyful nature of our mind. From there we can interact with mental objects with greater peace and ease on our own terms, from a position of mental strength. Gradually, the tightness of the grip of our grasping loosens, and mental objects transform into the four healing powers, the source of peace and joy.

If our mind is in peace, our emotions will be calm, the four elements of our body will be balanced, and the body's flow of energy circulation will be normal. Our relationships with others will be healthy and beneficial since whatever we say will be the words of peace. Our body's every expression will transmit peace.

In order to find and employ the healing power of our mind and the healing qualities of mental objects, we must consistently and repeatedly meditate on the four healing powers: positive images, positive words, positive feeling, and positive belief.

POSITIVE IMAGES: This is about seeing or visualizing images that we appreciate as a form with positive qualities. Most of the time, our minds are occupied with negative or neutral images. But if we build a habit of seeing or visualizing positive images, then these positive mental objects could awaken the peaceful and joyful nature of our mind spontaneously. Almost all of us, whenever we think, form mental images of whatever we are thinking about. The positive and negative qualities of our images invoke and feed joyful or painful concepts, emotions, and feelings in us all the time. So if we could get into the habit of seeing or visualizing images of religious significance or secular images that have a positive significance, such as a blossoming flower, we could use these images as a powerful source of healing to transform our minds and bodies.

POSITIVE WORDS: This is about thinking of or labeling our positive images with positive words. Positive images can become an even greater source of healing when we empower and magnify them with positive designations. Words or labeling are an integral part of formulating our thoughts. Whenever we think, commentaries, dialogues, and monologues are constantly running through our heads.

So, designate a positive image with a religious prayer or a secular word of positive significance such as "This is a totally beautiful flower." "It is colorful and blossoming." "How wonderful it is!" Repeating the positive words that amplify the positive qualities of the images magnifies their power to heal.

POSITIVE FEELING: This is about feeling the qualities of the positive objects mentally and physically. Letting ourselves really feel positive qualities heightens the force of healing. It goes beyond seeing and thinking of the positive object as inspiring. For example, by feeling the freshness, purity, and blossoming attributes of a flower within us, we take those qualities into a deep level of our mind and body.

POSITIVE BELIEF: This is about trusting in the healing power of meditating on positive images, words, and feelings. The point is not to develop blind faith, but to develop an experience of total comfort with the meditative experience that we are doing based upon our own gradual progress in the meditation. Developing unconditioned trust in healing fulfills the healing power of meditation.

The healing meditation here is based on Buddhism. Many Buddhist meditations are unique trainings specifically for Buddhists. But a greater part of its teachings are universal and beneficial to anyone eager to apply them. The meditative methods given here are those open for people of any faith, if their faith permits.

You should start the meditation by bringing the mind back

to the body in an atmosphere of peace and calmness. Sit still in a quiet place, closing your eyes, and breathing naturally.

Visualize a totally pure, open, and boundless sky in front of you. Think about and feel the quality of that sky. It brings a sense of clarity and openness, the quality of the sky in you.

Then in that open sky, visualize the image of the Blessed One, the Divine Presence. Many religions believe that the Blessed One is universal. It is within us and outside of us. However, for people who are used to being conceptual, dualistic, and having their needs fulfilled by higher sources, it is important to meditate and pray to the presence of a higher power as a source of healing. The higher source or Blessed One could be the Buddha, a saint, or a master—if your faith allows. See, think, feel, and believe from the bottom of your heart that this presence is the embodiment of omniscient wisdom, unconditioned love, and all-pervading power.

Then channel the energy of your devotion in the form of prayer to invoke the compassionate blessings of the Blessed One. It is not just words, but the joyful sound of your mind and the celebratory feeling of your heart joined by the sound of devotional power of the whole universe. The prayer could be any prayer, positive word, mantra, or just the sacred syllable, *ah. Ah* has a universal and open quality. According to Buddhism, it is the most profound word, the source and essence of all expressions.

As the result of prayer, think that blessings are coming toward you in the form of rainbow light-like beams. They merge into you. These lights are immaculate and have the qualities of all four elements—the strength of earth, the fluidity of water, the heat of fire, and the mobility of air. These beams are filled with the feelings of bliss and heat—blissful heat—the healing energies.

Think and feel that every cell of your body—from the top of your head to the soles of your feet—is filled with healing light, with healing energies. Its mere touch purifies and heals all the ills of your body and mind. Your body is transformed into a body of healing light with healing energies. Your mind is transformed into a mind of peace and joy. Your breathing becomes waves of healing energies and healing sounds that travel along the cells of your body.

From the Blessed One, the healing light with healing energies extends in all directions, healing every being and the entire universe. All of existence becomes a world of healing light with healing energies.

Finally, recognize and acknowledge whatever positive experience you felt as a result of the meditation. Then let your mind be

Through meditation, we can realize the awareness of the peaceful and joyful nature of our mind.

one with that particular experience, as if you have merged with it, like water pouring into water. Relax without thinking. Do this again and again. This helps bring the healing result to a deeper level of your consciousness and preserves it better.

Early morning is generally the best time to meditate, as your mind could still be in peace and your energy still calm. The best place is a solitary place. Whatever you pick, you should choose the best time and place that you can afford and feel good about. At the beginning, you should meditate for about an hour. Once you feel that you are well-rooted in the meditation, even five minutes a day will be a great source of well-being.

Like food, exercise, rest, and medicine, meditation is a very important component of healing and keeping healthy. Healing light dispels all mental and emotional darkness. Healing energies melt mental and physical tumors. Healing meditation loosens the tightness of the mental grip of grasping. It generates the strength of peace and joy. It balances the physical elements and normalizes the flow of circulation. It will not only ease the ills of your body and mind but also heal them from their roots—past mental and emotional tendencies. Once you are healthy, you can share the same with others.

MARTHA STEWART

TULKU THONDUP, an esteemed author and teacher, was born in East Tibet and studied at the famed Dodrupchen Monastery. In 1958 he settled in India, where he taught at Indian universities for many years. He came to the United States in 1980 as a visiting scholar at Harvard University. For the past two decades he has lived in Cambridge, Massachusetts, engaging in translation and writing on Tibetan Buddhism, particularly the Nyingma teachings, under the auspices of the Buddhayana Foundation. Among his books are *The Healing Power of Mind*, which has been published in seventeen languages, and *Boundless Healing*, published in twelve languages. For more information, visit www.tulkuthondup.com.

YOGA | Bringing Together Body and Mind

RICHARD FAULDS

Yoga and meditation are complementary practices. Yoga brings you to the meditation cushion relaxed and present. Meditation deepens your capacity for self-awareness, making your time on the yoga mat more mindful. While seen as distinct practices today, yoga and meditation have always been linked.

Yoga offers many benefits to meditators. For beginners, yoga helps release layers of chronic muscle tension that often make sitting still, breathing freely, and focusing the mind difficult. For regular meditators, yoga is a way to fine-tune the body-mind, creating a palpable sense of physical ease and mental balance that makes it easier to stay with and progress in your sitting practice. Advanced meditators often discover that a combination of yoga postures, deep breathing, and concentration can release energy blocks and awaken latent capacities, facilitating unexpected shifts in internal awareness that spill over into meditation practice.

When practiced with sensitivity, yoga is a meditative practice itself, an experience of mindfulness in motion in which awareness rests on the sensations arising from stretching and breathing. Yogic breathing, or *pranayama,* is an integral part of the practice, freeing up and smoothing out the flow of subtle energy through the nervous system, which eliminates mental agitation and prepares the yogi to transition easily into meditation. So is *yoga nidra,* or deep relaxation, which provides a way to transition out of meditation practice and return to life refreshed and rejuvenated.

YOGA PROGRAM

Yoga practice does not have to be time consuming. The three brief yoga sequences featured on the accompanying CD are designed to give you a taste of yoga's many benefits. The first two are meant to be done before you sit, either separately or together. The third will close your sitting practice with a sense of deep relaxation. Each includes a breathing exercise to accentuate the benefits. Please read through the following overview of the series before turning on the CD to practice.

OPENING YOGA POSES
Standing Series
One of the ways yoga works its magic is by flexing the spine through a range of movements. This not only allows you to regain good posture, but it also helps free the peripheral nerves that exit the spinal column of any pinching or pressure. This series begins with Standing Swinging Twist (also called Ringing the Temple Gong), includes Quarter Moon Pose, and ends with Standing Angle Bend.

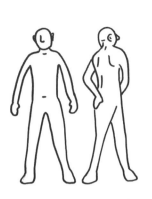

Standing Swinging Twist

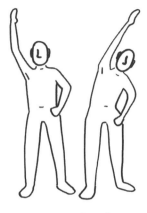
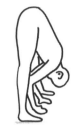

Quarter Moon Pose

Standing Angle Bend

Seated Side Stretch

Seated Twist

Seated Forward Bend

Sitting Series

This series includes three exercises: Seated Side Stretch, Seated Twist, and Seated Forward Bend. The instructions for each guide you to coordinate breath and motion, moving in and out of the stretch a few times before holding the posture for one or more deep breaths in and out.

While seen as distinct practices today, yoga and meditation have always been linked.

CLOSING YOGA POSES

The final track on the CD contains simple poses to help you integrate the effects of sitting meditation practice. It will guide you through Fingers to Toes Stretch, Lying Twist Pose, and Corpse Pose with Relaxing Breath, inhaling naturally and exhaling long, slow, and smooth. As the exhalations lengthen, you engage the relaxation response and activate the parasympathetic nervous system and all its healing mechanisms. Follow the instructions to relax various body parts; then let go into deep relaxation.

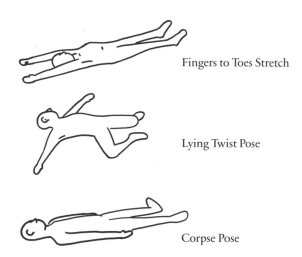

Fingers to Toes Stretch

Lying Twist Pose

Corpse Pose

RICHARD FAULDS has practiced yoga and meditation for twenty-five years in close association with Kripalu Center for Yoga & Health. The president of Kripalu from 1998 to 2001, he currently chairs the board of trustees and leads a variety of workshops and programs. Richard is the author of *Kripalu Yoga* and several other books on the Kripalu tradition. He lives with his wife, the poet Danna Faulds, in the Shenandoah Valley of Virginia. For more information, visit www.kripalu.org.

Frequently Asked Qutestions

How often should I meditate?
It's best to try to meditate a little bit everyday. Frequency is much more important than duration. Ten minutes a day every day is preferable to an hour every Sunday. If you don't have ten minutes, try to take a few moments on the bus on the way to work or before falling asleep at night to tune into your breath and let your mind relax. If you're stuck in traffic, it's not a good idea to meditate, but you can turn off the radio, shut down your cell phone, slow down, and let yourself enjoy the quiet.

What happens if I skip a day?
It's okay. Don't make yourself feel so guilty that you never want to practice again. Just return to it the next day.

What if I can't stop myself from thinking when I'm meditating?
It's impossible to stop thinking; this is what the mind does. It's very important to realize that meditation is not about clearing

the mind of all activity. It's about coming into a different, gentler, more playful relationship with your thoughts.

I'm busy from morning till night. How can I possibly make time for this practice?
Try several very short periods of meditation a day—five minutes or so. You could do this at your desk, on the bus, or anyplace you can sit quietly. You can connect with the mind of meditation for a minute, or even for a few seconds. Whenever you think of it, let your attention rest on your breath.

I have strong religious beliefs that have nothing to do with meditation. Will I have to give any of these up?
No. Buddhist meditation is nontheistic. You're not required to believe in any doctrine.

Meditation can get so boring. Am I doing something wrong?
The Tibetan teacher Chögyam Trungpa has said that boredom is actually a sign that things are going well—you are slowing down and connecting with stillness. Your mind is settling, and this is great. Stick with it, and see where it leads.

How do I know if I'm doing it right?
If you're continuing to practice and are remembering to follow the meditation instruction, everything is going fine.

People report all kinds of amazing experiences and insights, but I never have anything like this. Am I doing something wrong or missing something?
No. Everyone's experience of meditation is different. It is completely individual. In any case, the instruction for dealing with amazing experiences is the same as the instruction for thoughts: Gently let them go, and return to the practice.

What am I trying to accomplish?
Absolutely nothing. Meditating with a goal or in order to accomplish something is not giving the practice a fair shake. What is helpful is to let yourself off the hook, step off the self-improvement treadmill, and simply be with yourself in your natural state. The practice isn't about achieving something. It's about letting go.

What if my leg falls asleep or I have an itch? Can I move?
Yes, but move mindfully. Don't automatically shift or scratch.

First, bring your attention to the sensation and take it in. What does it really feel like? Then adjust as needed.

While I'm meditating, I often think of important things I have to do (for example, return a phone call or water the plants). When I think of something important, is it okay to stop meditating and make a list or something?

It's important to stay with the technique. Remember: All thoughts—good or bad, exciting or boring, important or silly— are to be released and attention returned to the breath. If something pops to mind that you want to be sure to remember, let it go. Commit yourself to the practice wholeheartedly.

I'm really loving this and want to share it with everyone in my family. Can I teach them how to meditate?

It's preferable to direct them to a meditation center for instruction from a meditation teacher. See page 111 for resources.

Instructions for Creating a Daily Practice

There are basically four things to consider if you'd like to begin a daily meditation practice.

ENVIRONMENT

Find a clean, quiet, relaxed spot to meditate. You can designate a room, a corner of a room, or even a particular chair for this purpose. Choose a spot that feels cheerful and even a bit elegant. All that is needed is a chair or cushion to sit on and a timer of some sort. If you'd like, you can light a candle or place a photo of something or someone inspiring nearby, but these things are not necessary. It's really easy to get lost in trying to create the perfect spot, so keep it simple.

TIMING

Try to practice at the same time each day. Most people find it simplest to meditate in the mornings, but anytime is good as long as you can make it regular. A routine helps solidify habit. At the same time, don't beat yourself up if you miss a day. (The only thing worse than not doing what you know you should is making yourself feel terrible about not doing what you know you should.)

PREPARATION

What would you guess are the biggest impediments to meditation practice? I assumed they were not having enough time or being unable to relax. According to meditation experts, however, forgetting the instructions is considered a classic obstacle. We don't forget because we're dumb, we just forget because we haven't ingrained the moves yet. It's like learning to play a piece of music. Learning it once doesn't guarantee that the next time you sit down to play, you'll remember all the details. It's the same with meditation. So it's really helpful to prepare by reviewing the instructions, either by running them down in your mind or rereading them in this or another book. In addition to refreshing your memory, before you practice, take a moment and say to yourself, "Now I'm going to practice meditation. During this time, everything can wait." Tell yourself this a few times before beginning your practice, or until you basically feel that it's true.

ATTITUDE

Okay, are you really, really sure you want to meditate for one hour every single day for the rest of your life? If so, carry on! But for most of us, this is too big a commitment to make before we even know what it's really like to meditate. Set an expectation for yourself that you know you can fulfill. For example, begin by committing to ten minutes, seven days a week for one month. This is challenging, but not impossible.

Again, consistency is more important than duration. Ten minutes a day is better than an hour once a week. But most important of all is to be kind to yourself. So when you make time to sit, relax, and when you fail to make time, you could also relax. Just try again.

RESOURCES

RECOMMENDED BOOKS

To learn more about the practices and teachers in *Quiet Mind,* the following books, videos, and audio programs are suggested.

Tibetan Buddhism and Shambhala Buddhism

Chödrön, Pema. *When Things Fall Apart.* Boston: Shambhala Publications, 1997.

———. *The Wisdom of No Escape and the Path of Loving-Kindness.* Boston: Shambhala Publications, 1991.

Dalai Lama and Howard C. Cutler. *The Art of Happiness: A Handbook for Living.* New York: Riverhead Books, 1998.

Davidson, Richard J. and Anne Harrington, eds. *Visions of Compassion: Western Scientists and Tibetan Buddhists Examine Human Nature.* New York: Oxford University Press, 2002.

Goleman, Daniel. *Destructive Emotions: A Scientific Dialogue with the Dalai Lama.* New York: Bantam Books, 2003.

Lief, Judith L. *Making Friends with Death: A Buddhist Guide to Encountering Mortality.* Boston: Shambhala Publications, 2001.

Mingyur, Yongey Rinpoche. *The Joy of Living: Unlocking the Secret and Science of Happiness.* New York: Harmony, 2007.

Sakyong, Mipham. *Ruling Your World: Ancient Strategies for Modern Life.* New York: Morgan Road Books, 2005.

_____. *Turning the Mind into an Ally.* New York: Riverhead Books, 2003.

Thondup, Tulku. *Boundless Healing: Meditation Exercises to Enlighten the Mind and Heal the Body.* Boston: Shambhala Publications, 2000.

_____. *Enlightened Journey: Buddhist Practice as Daily Life.* Boston: Shambhala Publications, 1995.

_____. *The Healing Power of the Mind: Simple Meditation Exercises for Health, Well-Being, and Enlightenment.* Boston: Shambhala Publications, 1996.

_____. *Peaceful Death, Joyful Rebirth: A Tibetan Buddhist Guidebook with a CD of Guided Meditations.* Boston: Shambhala Publications, 2005.

Trungpa, Chögyam. *Cutting Through Spiritual Materialism.* Boston: Shambhala Publications, 1987.

_____. *Shambhala: The Sacred Path of the Warrior.* Boston: Shambhala Publications, 1984.

Vipassana

Kabat-Zinn, Jon. *Wherever You Go, There You Are: Mindfulness Meditation in Everyday Life.* New York: Hyperion, 1994.

Rosenberg, Larry. *Breath by Breath: The Liberating Practice of Insight Meditation.* Boston: Shambhala Publications, 1998.

_____. *Living in the Light of Death: On the Art of Being Truly Alive.* Boston: Shambhala Publications, 2000.

Salzberg, Sharon. *Faith: Trusting Your Own Deepest Experience.* New York: Riverhead Books, 2002.

_____. *A Heart as Wide as the World: Living with Mindfulness, Wisdom, and Compassion.* Boston: Shambhala Publications, 1997.

_____. *Lovingkindness: The Revolutionary Art of Happiness.* Boston: Shambhala Publications, 1995.

Zen

Huber, Cheri. *Suffering Is Optional: 3 Keys to Freedom and Joy.* Murphys, Calif.: Keep It Simple Books, 2002.

Loori, John Daido. *Finding the Still Point: A Beginner's Guide to Zen Meditation with a CD of Guided Instructions.* Boston: Shambhala Publications, 2007.

Nhat Hanh, Thich. *Peace Is Every Step: The Path of Mindfulness in Everyday Life.* New York: Bantam Books, 1991.

Suzkui, Shunryu. *Not Always So: Practicing the True Spirit of Zen.* Edited by Edward Espe Brown. New York: HarperCollins, 2002.

_____. *Zen Mind, Beginner's Mind.* Boston: Shambhala Publications, 2006.

Yoga

Faulds, Richard. *Kripalu Yoga: A Guide to Practice On and Off the Mat.* New York: Bantam Books, 2006.

————, ed. *Sayings of Swami Kripalu: Inspiring Quotes from a Contemporary Yoga Master.* Kearney, Neb., Morris Publishing, 2004.

Of General Interest

Goleman, Daniel. *The Meditative Mind.* New York: Tarcher, 1988.

Tolle, Eckhart. *The Power of Now: A Guide to Spiritual Enlightenment.* Novato, Calif.: New World Library, 2004.

RECOMMENDED AUDIO

Adyashanti. *True Meditation.* Louisville, Colo.: Sounds True, 2006.

Chödrön, Pema. *Getting Unstuck: Breaking Your Habitual Patterns & Encountering Naked Reality.* Louisville, Colo.: Sounds True, 2004.

————. *Good Medicine: How to Turn Pain into Compassion with Tonglen Meditation.* Louisville, Colo.: Sounds True, 2001.

Kornfield, Jack. *Buddhist Meditation for Beginners.* Louisville, Colo.: Sounds True, 2006.

Sakyong, Mipham. *Ruling Your World: Ancient Strategies for Modern Life.* Boston: Shambhala Audio, 2007.

Salzberg, Sharon Salzberg and Joseph Goldstein. *Insight Meditation: An In-Depth Correspondence Course.* Louisville, Colo.: Sounds True, 2004.

MEDITATION CENTERS

If you find that you'd like to make meditation an ongoing part of your life, please seek instruction from an authorized teacher. Questions invariably arise, and it's important (not to mention practical) to get answers from trained practitioners.

Online Listings
To find a meditation center near you, visit:

www.shambhala.org (for shamatha meditation)
www.dharma.org (for vipassana meditation)
http://global.sotozen-net.or.jp/eng/regional_office_north_america
.html (for Soto Zen meditation)

Meditation Retreat Centers
These centers offer in-depth meditation (and other) programs:

Dai Bosatsu Zendo Kongo-Ji
Livingston Manor, N.Y.
www.daibosatsu.org

Green Gulch Farm
Muir Beach, Calif.
www.sfzc.org/ggf/

Esalen Institute
Big Sur, Calif.
www.esalen.org

Insight Meditation Society
Barre, Mass.
www.dharma.org/ims

Karmê Chöling
Barnet, Vt.
www.karmecholing.org

Kripalu Center for Yoga & Health
Lenox, Mass.
www.kripalu.org

Omega Institute
Rhinebeck, N.Y.
www.eomega.org

Shambhala Mountain Center
Red Feather Lakes, Col.
www.shambhalamountain.org

Spirit Rock Meditation Center
Woodacre, Calif.
www.spiritrock.org

Tassajara Zen Mountain Center
Carmel Valley, Calif.
www.sfzc.org/tassajara

DEDICATION OF MERIT

By this merit may all attain omniscience.
May it defeat the enemy, wrongdoing.
From the stormy waves of birth, old age, sickness, and death,
From the ocean of samsara, may I free all beings.

By the confidence of the golden sun of the great East,
May the lotus garden of the Rigden's wisdom bloom.
May the dark ignorance of sentient beings be dispelled.
May all beings enjoy profound, brilliant glory.

ABOUT SUSAN PIVER

VIDURA BARRIOS

Susan Piver is the *New York Times* best-selling author of *The Hard Questions: 100 Essential Questions to Ask Before You Say "I Do"* and *How Not to Be Afraid of Your Own Life,* which offers insight and information from Buddhism about conquering the fears that hold you back. She is a graduate of a Buddhist seminary and an authorized meditation instructor in the Shambhala Buddhist lineage. She is also the founder of Padma Media, a company that works with best-selling authors and publishers to create multimedia projects that support health and well-being.

Susan is a frequent contributor to *Body + Soul* and *Shambhala Sun* and is regularly featured in the media, including appearances on *Oprah,* the *Today* show, and CNN, and in *USA Today, The Wall Street Journal, Time, Money,* and others. For more information, visit www.susanpiver.com.

LIBRARY OF CONGRESS CATALOGING-IN-PUBLICATION DATA
Quiet mind: a beginner's guide to meditation / compiled by Susan Piver.
p.   cm.
Rev. and updated ed. of: Joyful mind. Rodale, c2002.
ISBN 978-1-59030-597-3 (hardcover: alk. paper)
1. Meditation—Buddhism. I. Piver, Susan, 1957– II. Joyful mind.
BQ5612.J69 2008
294.3'4435—dc22
2008015304

CD TRACK LIST

Meditations

Produced by Susan Piver. Edited by Susan Piver, Rick Rowe, and Geoff Thurber. Mastered at Heart Punch Studio, Boston.